The most important thing is to enjoy your life - to be happy - it's all that matters.

Audrey Hepburn

Be happy for this moment. This moment is your life.

Omar Khayyam

A birthday is just another day where you go to work and people give you love. Age is just a state of mind, and you are as old as you think you are. You have to count your blessings and be happy.

Abhishek Bachchan

You will never be happy if you continue to search for what happiness consists of. You will never live if you are looking for the meaning of life.

Albert Camus

Be happy with what you have and are, be generous with both, and you won't have to hunt for happiness.

William E. Gladstone

Trust yourself. Create the kind of self that you will be happy to live with all your life. Make the most of yourself by fanning the tiny, inner sparks of possibility into flames of achievement.

Golda Meir

I, not events, have the power to make me happy or unhappy today. I can choose which it shall be. Yesterday is dead, tomorrow hasn't arrived yet. I have just one day, today, and I'm going to be happy in it.

Groucho Marx

Be happy. It's one way of being wise.

Sidonie Gabrielle Colette

Happiness, true happiness, is an inner quality. It is a state of mind. If your mind is at peace, you are happy. If your mind is at peace, but you have nothing else, you can be happy. If you have everything the world can give - pleasure, possessions, power - but lack peace of mind, you can never be happy.

Dada Vaswani

How can a woman be expected to be happy with a man who insists on treating her as if she were a perfectly normal human being.

Oscar Wilde

We focus so much on our differences, and that is creating, I think, a lot of chaos and negativity and bullying in the world. And I think if everybody focused on what we all have in common - which is - we all want to be happy.

Ellen DeGeneres

Think of all the beauty still left around you and be happy.

Anne Frank

It's easy to impress me. I don't need a fancy party to be happy. Just good friends, good food, and good laughs. I'm happy. I'm satisfied. I'm content.

Maria Sharapova

Be happy with being you. Love your flaws. Own your quirks. And know that you are just as perfect as anyone else, exactly as you are.

Ariana Grande

Happiness is a choice. You can choose to be happy. There's going to be stress in life, but it's your choice whether you let it affect you or not.

Valerie Bertinelli

If someone decides they're not going to be happy, it's not your problem. You don't have to spend your time and energy trying to cheer up someone who has already decided to stay in a bad mood. Believe it or not, you can actually hurt people by playing into their self-pity.

Joyce Meyer

You must try to generate happiness within yourself. If you aren't happy in one place, chances are you won't be happy anyplace.

Ernie Banks

My theory on life is that life is beautiful. Life doesn't change. You have a day, and a night, and a month, and a year. We people change - we can be miserable or we can be happy. It's what you make of your life.

Mohammed bin Rashid Al Maktoum

Life is like a roller coaster, live it, be happy, enjoy life.

Avril Lavigne

I think most of us are raised with preconceived notions of the choices we're supposed to make. We waste so much time making decisions based on someone else's idea of our happiness - what will make you a good citizen or a good wife or daughter or actress. Nobody says, 'Just be happy - go be a cobbler or go live with goats.'

Sandra Bullock

It is really rare to find someone you really, really love and that you want to spend your life with and all that stuff that goes along with being married. I am one of those lucky people. And I think she feels that way too. So the romantic stuff is easy because you want them to be happy.

Harry Connick, Jr.

If you want to be happy, be.

Leo Tolstoy

I gave up my struggle with perfection a long time ago. That is a concept I don't find very interesting anymore. Everyone just wants to look good in the photographs. I think that is where some of the pressure comes from. Be happy. Be yourself, the day is about a lot more.

Anne Hathaway

If you want others to be happy, practice compassion. If you want to be happy, practice compassion.

Dalai Lama

Instead of being critical of people in authority over you and envious of their position, be happy you're not responsible for everything they have to do. Instead of piling on complaints, thank them for what they do. Overwhelm them with encouragement and appreciation!

Joyce Meyer

There are so many funny women in the world, and there has been for so many years, so I'll be happy when people can just move on from that, and things can just be 'comedies' and not 'female' or 'male,' and everyone gets an equal opportunity.

Kristen Wiig

Labor, under their current leadership, want to be the Downtown Abbey party when it comes to educational opportunity. They think working class children should stick to the station in life they were born into - they should be happy to be recognized for being good with their hands and not presume to get above themselves.

Michael Gove

I hate crowds of people pretending to be happy on one night of the year, where they get drunk and obnoxious by the end of the night.

Kenny Hickey

I don't really make plans and I just want to be happy and continue with my business and take care of my wife and kids. I want to sit back, relax and enjoy life.

Larry Holmes

If I can stand up when I'm 80, I'll be happy to cruise around on a skateboard. If I feel like my skills are fading, I just won't do it publicly.

Tony Hawk

I have to be happy in the here and now because every time you start focusing on your legacy you're really setting yourself up for disappointment.

Michael Bolton

Fortunately, I don't spend too much time reading or worrying about what people have to say, but the goal for me throughout this whole process - throughout my whole life - is to try to be happy.

Landon Donovan

Indeed it is possible to stand with one foot on the inevitable 'banana peel' of life with both eyes peering into the Great

Beyond, and still be happy, comfortable, and serene - if we will even so much as smile.

Douglas Fairbanks

There's just so many things I wanna do. At the end of the day, I wanna be happy.

Jessica Lowndes

All you need to do is turn on the news, and in five minutes, you're depressed with the state of the world. Choosing joy is a completely active choice. It doesn't just happen. You can't just say, 'I want to be happy.' You have to take action.

Billy Porter

One idea I explore in my stand-up show is whether, if you try looking at the universe rationally and avoid coping mechanisms like mysticism or religion, you can still be happy knowing you are going to die after a brief time on this spinning ball.

Robin Ince

I wrote for years before I was ever published, and I don't think I could ever stop. That said, I was also a veterinarian before I sold my first book, and I still volunteer my time to help with animal welfare causes. So that is a career I would be happy to return to - while still secretly writing strange stories back in my doctor's office.

James Rollins

I want to be able to fly like a superhero. I won't be happy until I can fly across oceans and cities, saving people from being murdered.

Heather Graham

A person may rightfully be happy if in this life he could do a great favor for widows and orphans, could assist support than, and facilitate fate of people.

Islom Karimov

You have to be in love with yourself before anyone else can fall in love with you; to be happy with yourself.

Lily Allen

What could an unsanctified man do in Heaven, if by any chance he got there? Let that question be fairly looked in the face and fairly answered. No man can possibly be happy in a place where he is not in his element and where all around him is not congenial to his tastes, habits and character.

J. C. Ryle

I'm a character actress. I'm the girl next door, the aunt, the quirky cousin. You have to innately know who you are and be happy with that.

Faith Prince

I've learned that I have to be happy with creating discussion and debate and that I shouldn't be trying to write a book that appeals to the consensus.

Miguel Syjuco

I want to be happy. I realized that being happy isn't necessarily about getting there, it's how you get there. It almost sounds like a cliche, but every entrepreneur I've talked to - every good entrepreneur - really enjoys the 'how you get here.'

Ben Huh

I would be happy if they just gave out nominations and there weren't any Oscars. But winning them is definitely an experience - to get up there and make a speech. Every film is hard work, and a few lucky people do get Oscars for what they do, and it's recognition for all that hard work on a certain level.

Walter Murch

There is one thing in this good old world that is positively sure - happiness is for all who strive to be happy - and those who laugh are happy. Everybody is eligible - you - me - the other fellow. Happiness is fundamentally a state of mind - not a state of body.

Douglas Fairbanks

I believe as musicians and artists we have an obligation to our souls. What that is? Only each one of us knows. I can speak for myself and say my obligation is to be happy. When I'm happy, I make great music. When I'm unhappy and my heart is broken, I may make brokenhearted music, but it still sounds good.

Narada Michael Walden

I don't think I'd be happy if I were satisfied. I enjoy challenge, and I wouldn't say that I'm an ambitious person career-wise or financially, really. I would like to travel more comfortably, but that's really about all I need.

Jason Isbell

If readers, young and old, would take even a moment to reflect on our rapidly shifting culture and ideology, I would be happy. Many leaders of the older generation dismiss emerging culture. Those leaders are at risk of becoming a feeble voice-piece without followers. Most of the younger generation is going deaf to the truth.

Ted Dekker

You've got to be happy when you play a sad character; otherwise, you just get depressed. Make your real life as fun as possible.

Sophie Turner

I always believed no matter where you are, as long as you're doing what you love doing, you're going to be happy.

Roberto Alomar

I want to do good, and I want people to be happy, and sometimes when you're a people pleaser, you spread yourself too thin.

Tika Sumpter

One should always be happy, irrespective of what you achieve in a match or in life. That's how I live my life.

Virender Sehwag

To me, acting is acting... I'd be happy working on a street corner in a mime troupe.

Kelly McGillis

You have to be happy with yourself first of all - that's the most important thing.

Aly Michalka

I don't think you'll ever be happy about anything unless you've done it.

Gary Barlow

Once I said to my mother: 'You would be happy if I just kept well-dressed and had good manners,' and she said: 'What else is there?'

Cy Twombly

We live in a flat; my wife would be happy if we had a house with stairs. Or a little cottage in the country.

Fergus Henderson

When I first came into the business, I had to, for the sake of being able to sell myself as an artist, always be happy and jovial and smiling. I was the happy nice girl, and I am the happy nice girl, but I have my moments, too.

Kelly Price

When I look for the next project, it's always about, 'Is it going to push me out of my comfort zone? Am I doing something different? Am I working with people who are passionate about what they're doing?' At the end of the day, if I'm going to be bored on set, then I'm not gonna be happy.

Amanda Crew

The Soul of man is made an article of merchandize by his fellow man and can such a land be happy? No! Happyness does not dwell in any land that is scard by the blighting curse of Slavery.

Ezra Cornell

Most of my actor friends don't believe it's possible to let go of it and be happy, and for a while that was true for me. For the first two years I ached, every day. And I had such bad dreams. But then I made the decision to start working on my little shop and all that went away.

Genie Francis

If you try to hold on to something you don't have anymore, you can't be happy in the moment.

Jennifer Grey

You can be right or you can be happy.

Gerald Jampolsky

We must select the illusion which appeals to our temperament, and embrace it with passion, if we want to be happy.

Cyril Connolly

Making love in the morning got me through morning sickness. I found I could be happy and throw up at the same time.

Pamela Anderson

I don't need many things. I don't need glamour and attention to be happy. I'm very happy being settled and working my butt off and trying to win grand slams.

Maria Sharapova

Borders had lousy management and made bad corporate decisions, so its fate is less like a terrible accident than a slow-motion slide into a ditch, but it's hard to be happy about a bookseller's demise.

Susan Orlean

Some people just aren't meant to be happy.

Anna Torv

Most of us function under the model we have to get something in order to do something, in order to be something. If this happens, then I will be happy. And I'm suggesting to you that we live our entire lives based on that model, and that model is fundamentally flawed.

Srikumar Rao

Of course a woman who decides to work full time as a mother in the home can be happy and deserves full respect from us. Motherhood is one of the most challenging and creative jobs anyone can do. The goal is to remake the world so that our choices are not so stark.

Naomi Wolf

I want to build something I'd be happy to be employed by 10 years out.

David Karp

People are easily intimidated when they decorate their home. They think it has to be one way. But there's no one way. It's your way, your style. At the end of the day, you have to live there. It's your cocoon, your nest. You have to be happy in it.

Bryan Batt

I can choose to be happy, or choose to be miserable every day - waiting until I die.

Angel Haze

If you can be well without health, you may be happy without virtue.

Edmund Burke

I think happiness is a goal all of us can agree on. Let's face it - we all would like to be happy.

Joyce Meyer

We are more interested in making others believe we are happy than in trying to be happy ourselves.

Francois de La Rochefoucauld

As men are not able to fight against death, misery, ignorance, they have taken it into their heads, in order to be happy, not to think of them at all.

Blaise Pascal

I used to let other people's struggles affect my happiness. If they weren't happy, there was no way I was going to be happy.

The opposite was also true: If I wasn't happy, I didn't want anyone around me to be happy.

Joyce Meyer

Allow children to be happy in their own way, for what better way will they find?

Samuel Johnson

To be happy, we must be true to nature and carry our age along with us.

William Hazlitt

We must be doing something to be happy.

William Hazlitt

Want to raise children who will be happy adults? Teach them not to whine.

Dennis Prager

Remember that as a teenager you are in the last stage of your life when you will be happy to hear the phone is for you.

Fran Lebowitz

To live we must conquer incessantly, we must have the courage to be happy.

Henri Frederic Amiel

There is an hour wherein a man might be happy all his life, could he find it.

George Herbert

I think most artists would be happy to have bigger audiences rather than smaller ones. It doesn't mean that they are going to change their work in order necessarily to get it, but they're happy if they do get it.

Brian Eno

I just want my children to be happy. I want my children to be healthy.

Ricky Martin

I'll be happy if I can just stay out of Nebraska.

Dick Cavett

If you want to be happy, make others happy!

Dada Vaswani

I can go out raw with nothing, and my fans would still be happy, but I feel that I owe it to them to give them almost like a Broadway musical at this point in my life. I have to give them something more, so I do have to think of different ways to do it.

Mary J. Blige

To be happy is only to have freed one's soul from the unrest of unhappiness.

Maurice Maeterlinck

When you're miserable, you don't want anyone around you to be happy.

Amy Lee

You know, everybody knows some of what politicians say is malarkey, and having somebody there to call them on it is good. I'd be happy to do that any time and any place.

Elizabeth Edwards

To be happy when you are travelling, you need to be happy inside before you leave. A positive frame of mind will definitely enhance your travelling experience. If I'm not in a positive frame of mind then the whole thing definitely becomes more of a challenge for me.

Andrea Bocelli

In a creative business, if you're happy, it will come out in your work. I don't see how you can be happy if you don't like the people you're working with and if they aren't a joy to have fun with.

Christian Louboutin

My mother once said to me, 'You must promise to be happy; it is the greatest favour you can do to others'. It has guided me throughout my life.

Stephane Hessel

If I tell a man he needs to quit his soul-sucking job, he has to go home and fight with his wife or fight with his parents and fight with his in-laws and fight with everybody, because men aren't supposed to be happy; they're supposed to do well.

Martha Beck

My passion is doing movies, and as long as I keep doing that, I'll be happy. I want to do movies, fun roles and dramatic ones. I love all of it.

Vanessa Hudgens

Your parents would not be happy if you came home and said you wanted to grow up to be a chef or a rock star.

Jose Andres Puerta

I got a lot of problems, but I'm really good at intuiting what I need to do to be happy with whatever I create. I know when to stop myself, I know when to start, I know when to leave something alone. I guess I just kind of indulge that completely, and so I just take my time.

Fiona Apple

I am very much interested in getting parents to read to children, and trying to get people mentoring children. If I can do both I'll be happy.

Walter Dean Myers

It's the ultimate goal every day you wake up, to be happy. At the end of the week, you want to be happy. Happy in love, happy in work, happy in life, happy with yourself. It's pretty simple.

Pierce Brosnan

I'd be happy to provide advice if anybody asked me no matter who the President is.

Michael Bloomberg

We all want to be happy. We need to expand the notion of what that means, to make it bigger and wiser.

Sharon Salzberg

If I win, I'll take my wife and buy her a whole new wardrobe. If she's happy then I'll be happy.

Chris Daughtry

I love good and pleasure, I hate evil and pain, I want to be happy and I am not mistaken in believing, that people, angels and even demons have those same inclinations.

Nicolas Malebranche

I'm not going to do a song that's really sad and thoughtful. Although I've done ballads like 'Dear Darlin',' I want to make them dance and be happy.

Olly Murs

I have given up trying to be happy. It is no use an leads to nothing.

Anna Held

To be happy is, I guess, the most important thing in life.

Mary, Crown Princess of Denmark

I would be happy with an Olympic bronze. What I don't have is an Olympic medal.

Paula Radcliffe

I didn't want kids to think that to be happy, they had to be famous or rich or live in the big city.

Dan Savage

All I want is to live a peaceful life, to regain my life and be happy.

Mickey Rooney

I want my ex-wife and children to be happy.

Scott Weiland

Our fans want us to be happy and if that means being married or having a girlfriend, they are okay with that. Of course, in this industry it is a bit harder to have normal relationships, but it is possible.

A. J. McLean

'A Guide To Recognizing Your Saints' was the first real actor-actor part I did, and I hope I to do more. Action movies are fun, but I'd be happy not to do them if there are better roles.

Channing Tatum

I think we should all live the moment. But you also have to think ahead. You have to think, 'Am I going to be happy with this five, ten years from now? Is it going to let me evolve and grow, or am I going to grow to one day wish I had never done it?' Sometimes you just have to think a little bit ahead.

Gloria Estefan

My hardest thing was to let go, to be happy for everybody and just to enjoy. And go back to being what you were before you became an artist, and that was just a fan.

Garth Brooks

If you want to be happy, live discreetly. Does that make sense in English?

Olivier Martinez

There's this really good line in 'Women in Love' where Ursula says, 'I always thought it was a sin to be unhappy.' And actually I think that's very common, it's what a lot of people feel - that you have an obligation to life to be happy if you can.

Rachel Cusk

It's hard for me to be happy because I'm always worried about something going awry or what could happen to screw it up. It's hard for me to sit and look around, going, 'Ah, I'm really happy.' I'm not that kind of person.

Lisa Marie Presley

I don't do impersonations. I can do a wounded elephant! I can do a really good cow! And because of the amount of time I spent in North Yorkshire, I do a variety of sheep. All of which I will be happy to roll out for you!

Patrick Stewart

I want to be happy and stable. My life is clearly going to slow down.

Nicole Richie

My father worked hard, but we were still very poor; and I didn't want anybody arguing about money, so I became the entertainer - the one who wanted everyone to be happy. I didn't want there to be any problems.

Diana Ross

When my son was growing up, I was always guilty, no matter what I did. Make decisions and be happy with the decisions you've made. I tell myself, in the long run, it's the love, the quality of relationships that you have with your family, your friends and giving back to the community that matters.

Padmasree Warrior

An ordinary man can surround himself with two thousand books and thenceforward have at least one place in the world in which it is possible to be happy.

Augustine Birrell

Happiness is the first principle of life. Happiness basically means well-being. It is always good and always a choice... We need to make the choice to be happy in a particular situation, just as it is, and at a given moment.

Alexandra Stoddard

I've realised I can be happy.

Kevin Pietersen

I don't mind if the couple next to me is tense or the kids are whiny. I'd even be happy to hear an honest argument, evidence of thinking. I'd like to know these teeth-perfect families don't just buy each other stuff but just occasionally can talk to one another.

Margaret Heffernan

Phones and soundtracks and Muzak and fountains replace genuine and unpredictable human contact with a seamless soundtrack from a bad movie and a cliche that makes us believe we must all be happy.

Margaret Heffernan

I have a pretty active presence on social networking sites, and every day there are messages from so many young girls telling me that they are happy B-Town has curvy women like me. I feel you should be happy the way you are. Of course, fitness is important, but not to the extent of obsession!

Sonakshi Sinha

I don't see any of my colleagues as rivals. I don't think our generation needs to do that. We are a chilled out lot, and we should all be happy.

Shahid Kapoor

Any writer will be happy and good only if they know what they're doing and why they're doing it.

Yann Martel

I know conventional wisdom has always been to go to Europe, and I did that early on, and I tried it, but I realised pretty quickly if I wasn't playing, nothing else mattered - I wasn't going to be happy.

Landon Donovan

I suppose I'm happy when I know I've given a horse a good ride, no matter where it is. I like playing golf in the summer; I'm happy when I hit a good shot, and I enjoy watching Arsenal playing beautiful football, but overall I can't believe you can be happy when you're not winning. I honestly can't accept that.

Tony McCoy

There are but two places where all go after death, white and black, rich and poor; those places are Heaven and Hell. Heaven is a place made for those, who are born again, and who love God, and it is a place where they will be happy for ever.

Jupiter Hammon

I never wanted to do something grotesque. I never wanted to shock. I wanted my audience to be happy, to be kind.

Eva Zeisel

The only luck I had in my life was when I married you. I knew it wouldn't last because I was too happy. I knew they would not let me be happy.

Eddie Slovik

The No. 1 question I get from everybody is, 'How did you make it?' I'm like, Don't worry about making it. There is no making it. Just be happy.

Carson Daly

I've done a lot of things in a business where you're lucky to stay alive, so when the time comes, I'll be happy to pass my knowledge along and help someone else.

Felix Baumgartner

I've found that when the market's going down and you buy funds wisely, at some point in the future you will be happy.

Peter Lynch

I honestly think I'm just an actor. It doesn't matter the medium. I can go on stage and be happy, I can be on TV and be happy.

Michael Ealy

Be happy or die.

Rob Cohen

If God is in a life, it doesn't have to be big to be happy and to be important in His kingdom.

Keith Miller

Ever since I was a kid, I've always thought it very important to be happy inside. There's a lot of bad things happening in the world, but it's important to try to stay happy and appreciate what you've got, and don't look externally for the happiness.

Ana Ivanovic

What is happy? I think happy's in the moment. I don't think everybody can be happy all the time.

Shelby Lynne

I used to think drinking was the only way to be happy. Now I know there is no way to be happy.

Laura Kightlinger

You should learn to be happy with what you have. Besides, the fact that I'm not a huge star has allowed me to pick and choose the roles I want to do, not the ones some person sitting in a studio office thinks I should do.

Aidan Quinn

For me, the times in my life when I've been single have been more formative and crucial than I could have imagined. I can cope, function and be happy on my own. I'm highly capable. That doesn't mean I don't like being with a partner, or that I don't feel more rounded when I'm with someone. But the times on my own have been so good.

Lesley Manville

I will be happy with certainly when the corruption index improve.

Abdullah Ahmad Badawi

I'm going to give away a lot more than half my money. I'd be happy to give that to the government if the government put together programs that were like I'm giving away to charity, in which I believe the money is effectively used to help people.

Ray Dalio

I just want to get on stage and sing and be happy.

Ronnie Spector

As we depend upon our masters, for what we eat and drink and wear, and for all our comfortable things in this world, we cannot be happy, unless we please them.

Jupiter Hammon

Sure, one can always get the students to relax and be happy - entertained, but although being laid back and relax can also lead to creativity, mostly it means that nothing much gets done.

Donald Norman

If you're black, if you're gay, if you're Latin - we're all the same. We're all the same, and we all want the same: We want to be happy.

Kate del Castillo

I tell myself, 'If I can wake up each day and be excited about what I'm doing, then I must be happy.' But then again, maybe I'm in denial.

Alexandra Cassavetes

I could be happy doing something like architecture. It would involve another couple of years of graduate school, but that's what I studied in college. That's what I always wanted to do.

Parker Stevenson

I want to be happy going to work. I want to do a show I'm proud of.

Rob Thomas

We only have two things that we share in this life; we are born and we die. And what we do in between those times, we've got to be happy. I don't let the outside world deter me.

Dawn Fraser

I like loud music. I like music that fills my ears. I'm just going to pull out my iPod and see what we got here. We're always interested in new bands because we have a retail store in northern California. I think it's got to be happy.

Tyler Florence

I'd be happy if people said that I did a little bit to raise the dignity and recognition of the greatness of African-American music.

Ahmet Ertegun

Basically, I would be happy with any profession where I got to be creative and make things.

Christopher Paolini

You can't be happy if you're not tolerably happy with yourself. The addition of friends adds immeasurably to life.

Patrick O'Brian

It's an unhealthy habit to say that life is what you make of it, and if you want to be happy, then you can be happy. That's just rubbish, basically.

Mike Leigh

I mean, I can actually say goodbye to the game of golf, never hit another golf shot the rest of my life and I'd be happy because I can get back in life without any rotation.

Greg Norman

Winning is very important to me. I wouldn't be happy with anything less. And I work towards my goal.

Nafisa Joseph

Happiness was not made to be boasted, but enjoyed. Therefore tho others count me miserable, I will not believe them if I know and feel myself to be happy; nor fear them.

Thomas Traherne

If I can stay constantly busy, I'll be happy.

Daniel Cudmore

No matter how bad things are, you can at least be happy that you woke up this morning.

D. L. Hughley

The question I wanted to answer was, could I train my mind to be happy the same way one trains one's body?

Stefan Sagmeister

I want to be happy; why do I do things that make me unhappy?

Paul Schrader

This hearing came about very quickly. I do have a few preliminary comments, but I suspect you're more interested in asking questions, and I'll be happy to respond to those questions to the best of my ability.

David Kay

I wouldn't be happy had I only been a teacher, if all I had done was help young people, frankly. I don't get nearly the joy teaching as I do out of creation.

Barry Hannah

The popular notion is that Americans are addicted to fossil fuels, but I find that's not true; most people would be happy to power their lives with anything else.

Bill McKibben

Writers are too neurotic to ever be happy.

Connie Willis

When I first moved out to Los Angeles I was thinking, you know, I wanted to be an actor but I didn't really know what acting was about. I thought if I could be a model, or even do commercials and stuff like that for the rest of my life, I'd be happy.

Michael Biehn

I don't think I could be happy as an actor if there was a tyrant on the set.

David Warner

Henceforth, we shall be happy to be a free citizen in an independent country.

Bao Dai

If I never saw another airport again, I'd be happy!

Emm Gryner

Being a wife and a mother is very gratifying, but it's not a creative expression and that's something I need to be happy.

Genie Francis

I hope to live long and be happy. But I'd like to be remembered as somebody who did good rather than mischief.

Mary Archer

People want to be happy, so they don't want to feel as though they're mired in this world of ugliness. I think that if people can recognize that you can actually help and change that ugliness, then you'll feel a lot better about yourself as well, and that does create a certain amount of happiness.

Sheryl WuDunn

I'm definitely a people pleaser. I like people to be happy around me and be comfortable. I go out of my way, sometimes to a fault, to make sure everyone is okay.

Ken Jeong

Even if there's controversy, I'm going to make the decision, and people are going to be happy in one instance and unhappy in the next. But that's the job I've been given and the job I'm going to embrace.

Gina McCarthy

The only way to be happy and be a more enjoyable person to be around is to embrace what you've got. Everyone has issues about their body, but I feel confident now. I'm healthy and happy.

Mischa Barton

Every body about me seem'd happy but every body seem'd in a hurry to be happy somewhere else.

Hannah Cowley

Performing live actually thrills me. Just get me a stage, get me a mic, and I'm going to be happy.

Rita Wilson

If all else fails and you don't know what to wear, put on a black dress, and you'll be happy.

Lily Donaldson

I spend most of my time at the ranch with my family, and enjoy life - watch the sun come up, watch it go down, thank God for another day, and just be happy.

Marcus Luttrell

My allegiance was always to the act. I wanted them to be happy. I wasn't owned by a magazine or a record label. And I was a very naughty boy to boot!

Mick Rock

You have to make difficult choices in your life, and you just have to be happy with them.

Lori Loughlin

I have a very optimistic view of my future right now. I'm very excited to see where it goes, but I try not to make plans just because I know how unpredictable life can be. Especially the life of an actor, and especially the life of an actor on 'Glee.' I just want to be happy and healthy and surrounded by people I love, as cheesy as it sounds.

Melissa Benoist

I'm not the kind of person who sits off by myself and ignores everyone. I like to be happy!

Jenna Boyd

I would be happy to be labeled as a writer of offbeat stories. I don't know how to do anything else.

Caroline Thompson

To be happy, to make other people happy, to get into movie production more and probably to give some other people the chances that I had, to carry on enjoying being a mum and never to stop having flowers bought for me. I've still got a long way to go.

Sharon Stone

I mean, I am still such the-good-girl. I want everybody to like me. I want everybody to be happy.

Michelle Williams

I'd be happy to have regular face-to-face meetings at Downing Street with David Cameron to argue the case for alternative economic policies.

Frances O'Grady

I don't trust the Bee Gee's because there's no way they could always be happy.

Jon Crosby

After I can be happy with knowing that I did what I wanted to do.

Namie Amuro

It was a myth that's often perpetuated at commencement that holds that only hope and promise lie beyond the halls of academe. Don't worry, be happy. Everything is fine.

Paul Tsongas

There's not enough money in the world to get me singing 'Because We Want To' again. I wouldn't do it. I think Beyonce Knowles got a couple of million for a private show but I would be happy to turn it down.

Billie Piper

Television is a very writer-driven business, and it's one of the few parts of entertainment where writers are treated with respect, only because they need you. If they didn't have to treat you with respect, they would be happy to dismiss you.

Mitchell Hurwitz

I wish I had it in my power to furnish you with accommodation I should feel proud to do it, shall be happy to hear from you at anytime when you engagements will allow you an hour and remain with best wishes for yourself, family and circuit.

John Hawley

I would always be happy to serve my country in any way that I was called upon to do.

Mitt Romney

I wouldn't push my kids to do anything. I want them to be happy, healthy, and I want them to be who they want to be, you know?

Heidi Klum

When I first ran for Congress, I went to my daughter Alexandra, who was going to be a senior in high school, and said: 'I have a chance to run. I may not win, but I'd be gone three nights a week. So, if you want me to stay, I'll be happy to.' And do you know what she said to me? 'Mother, get a life!'

Nancy Pelosi

If I can wake up everyday before I die and know that I don't have to serve anyone food or drinks, I will be happy!

Kelly Clarkson

You can't just tell actors, especially young ones, to 'act happy' and expect them to do it. They must in some essential way be happy.

Roger Ebert

You cannot be happy with your family while being personally unhappy with your work. It's a Catch-22 kind of thing.

Mikhail Baryshnikov

If I die on a film set when I'm 80, I'll be happy with that.

Daniel Radcliffe

I'm not a greedy man; there really is nothing I couldn't live without. But if there was a fire, and I saved my child and my pets, I'd be happy.

Kid Rock

I think it's okay to feel jealous, but it's how you deal with it that's the important thing. You have to be happy for your friends when they do well because you want them to do well. It's not a competition.

Carrie Underwood

Am I being typecast as a horrible person? I don't know. I don't think so. But if it happens, I'd rather get to play that, because there's nothing fun about being sweet. Sweet can be so boring, so I'd be happy staying away from that.

January Jones

I think it's the same simple thing for everyone - to be happy, and have love in your life.

Juliette Binoche

I don't give away my shoes to celebrities for free. I'm only happy when people like what I do and make the effort to buy them. I would not be happy to see people in my shoes if I knew that they had to be paid to do it, that they had to be pushed.

Christian Louboutin

I would never share my daughter's wardrobe. Every five years you have to go through your wardrobe and say, 'This is possible, this is not possible.' But you have to be happy with yourself.

Carine Roitfeld

My students often say, 'My roommate read this story and really liked it,' and it's hard to convince them that there are things wrong with it. I say, 'Well, people who love you want you to be happy. But I'm your professor and I'm supposed to be teaching you something.'

Joyce Carol Oates

My passion is doing movies, so as long as I keep doing that I will be happy.

Vanessa Hudgens

All I wanted was to be straight so my parents could be happy.

Maurice Sendak

You can't write masterpieces in your 80s and be happy too.

Maurice Sendak

One is a child when one has a child. No one says, 'You will never be the same again.' Which is the truth! And we're all supposed to be happy all the time. What is that about?

Emma Thompson

I was kind of raised with the suggestion that I had a duty to do; that life was real, life was earnest. And I hated that, actually. I needed to be liberated, to be told that I could live the life that I wanted to live; that I didn't need a job, or to be shouted at; that I could be myself; that I could be happy.

Paul Theroux

All I wanted was to be straight so my parents could be happy. They never, never, never knew.

Maurice Sendak

The slave may be happy, but happiness is not enough.

Herbert Read

I do not need a lot of money to be happy.

Debra Winger

It's very hard to get the dynamics where two people can stimulate each other and be happy.

Elizabeth Hurley

Many blue-collar families struggling to pay rent would be happy to skip paying optional union dues.

Kevin O'Leary

I don't take myself very seriously. I like to make people laugh. You know, it's like, if a woman can't be happy for another woman's work, they have to go work on that.

Sharon Stone

I sort of look at some peers of mine and I think, 'No, you've got it all wrong!' I just want to tell them all to have babies and be happy and not get sucked into that Hollywood thing.

Gwyneth Paltrow

I'd be happy to stay single now because I've always been in relationships. For the first time ever I can do what I want, when I want, with who I want, without answering to anyone.

Carol Vorderman

For my part, if the audience wanted to see Dracula again, I would be happy to reprise the role. It is an immortal character that can appear anywhere because it lies beyond time. Possibilities are endless.

Luke Evans

I am a genius. Then it amused me to keep saying so, but now it does not. I expected to be happy sometime. Now I know I shall never be.

Mary MacLane

There are people who have energy that say 'don't come near me, don't get too close.' There's people like Adrienne Shelley who have the energy of 'come over here and give me a hug and if you're around me you're going to be happy about it.'

Nathan Fillion

I think you can be happy and still be competitive. A good lesson for everybody is to think a bit before you speak and represent who you really are instead of the brash emotional you.

Danica Patrick

I don't even have a small boat. I don't even have a toy boat in my bathtub. I don't have a biplane, I don't have anything. Those things are toys, and I don't need them to be happy.

Mo Ibrahim

How great is it to just rest and be happy and not move when you don't have to.

James Altucher

What the purpose of my life is about is I want to become the kind of person that God wants me to become, and through my study of the scriptures, I can articulate the kind of person that God would be happy if I become.

Clayton Christensen

Give me the whole world to run and then I'll be happy. If tomorrow I was told I had to sort out the whole world's problems I'd sleep like a baby.

Ken Livingstone

It's hard to say no to your kid. It's hard for them to stomp off and not be happy with you for an hour.

Martina McBride

I need freedom to be happy.

Johnny Weissmuller

If I'm breathing in 2016, I'll be happy.

Andrew Cuomo

I hope children will be happy with the books I've written, and go on to be readers all of their lives.

Beverly Cleary

It's no fun to be a struggling young actor. It's a desperate thing, no way to be happy. If you have any alternative, you should take it.

Tommy Lee Jones

Chefs are artists, and I couldn't be happy with my art if I was forced to use cheap ingredients.

Nobu Matsuhisa

It's a constant battle for everybody, but you need to be happy with yourself.

Gina Carano

I could go off into the wilderness and write fantasy novels for the rest of my life and probably be happy; but I always want to challenge myself.

Felicia Day

Well, here's the thing with relationships on 'True Blood': Once they happen then you have to throw a monkey-wrench into them, because to have people be happy is not that exciting.

Alan Ball

It's hard to be happy when you are facing 120 to 140 degree temperatures and nothing seems to be moving in a direction that you think or they think or you've been told it's supposed to be moving in.

Janis Karpinski

'Eureka' was very bad timing. The early 1980s: Reagan and Thatcher were in, greed was good, and here was a film about the richest man in the world who still couldn't be happy. Politically and sociologically, it was out of step.

Nicolas Roeg

As long as I am given the opportunity to keep performing and keep exploring in whatever medium, I'll be happy. As long as I get to spend time with my family, I'll be happy. As long as I can write in some form, I'll be happy. It is the essential things like that I equate with happiness.

Dan Stevens

I have my own worries and concerns and frustrations, but I'm doing something I love to do. My wife and kids are in good shape. What is there not to be happy about?

Chris O'Donnell

I think people who are not rich can be extremely happy. And I think the chances to be happy in this new world - with many more opportunities to be creative, to be online, to educate yourself - there'll be a lot more chances to be happy. It's not to say everyone will take them, but there will be a lot of new paths to opportunity.

Tyler Cowen

I would not be happy to do what I do unless I felt that the large audience wanted it.

Giorgio Moroder

I'm going to be like Benjamin Button; I'm just going to grow younger. I will probably be happy, fat, with kids and looking back and thinking, 'I was such a angry young woman.'

Lykke Li

If I have 1% of my dad's brain, I'll be happy. He's so quick.

Tamara Ecclestone

Whatever you do, be happy with you. Don't conform. You are who you are, and you shouldn't change that for anybody.

Aimee Teegarden

I want just to be happy and peaceful. And that's not always the case when you're married.

Olivier Martinez

Even if it's not what you planned, you can make a life for yourself on your own and be happy.

Lisa Scottoline

I'd be happy to live till 80 as long as I was comfortable and in good health. Mind you, ask me again on the eve of my 80th birthday. Even so, I hope we don't all start living to be 120. I'm not sure I'd cope with another 60 years.

Bonnie Tyler

I'd be happy doing anything on a film set.

Nick Frost

I need to write to be happy.

Nora Roberts

I did not know what it was to be happy for a whole day at a time, scarcely for an hour.

Georg Brandes

I think when I was 12, I started reading Evelyn Waugh, and I loved Evelyn Waugh so much, and I thought: 'This is how the world really is. If I could be Evelyn Waugh, then I would be happy.'

Candace Bushnell

It's such a luxury to be able to be happy about going to work in the morning.

Joe Pantoliano

I just wanted to be married and to be happy ever after.

Moira Kelly

I can't laugh, be happy, present myself at any prize and also win on the centre court.

Gabriela Sabatini

I like to be happy when I'm writing. If not, then how will the reader manage?

Kevin Barry

Things don't weigh me down any more. I confront things, and I move on. I don't dwell on things; I don't let things simmer under the surface. I am where it starts and where it ends. I have the power in my life to be happy.

Ricki-Lee Coulter

The purpose of our lives is to be happy.

Dalai Lama

Don't wait around for other people to be happy for you. Any happiness you get you've got to make yourself.

Alice Walker

You know it's love when all you want is that person to be happy, even if you're not part of their happiness.

Julia Roberts

Dedicate yourself to the good you deserve and desire for yourself. Give yourself peace of mind. You deserve to be happy. You deserve delight.

Hannah Arendt

Now and then it's good to pause in our pursuit of happiness and just be happy.

Guillaume Apollinaire

As a real person, he wouldn't last a minute, would he? But drama is about imperfection. And we've moved away from the aspirational hero. We got tired of it, it was dull. If I was House's friend, I would hate it. How he so resolutely refuses to be happy or take the kind-hearted road. But we don't always like morally good people, do we?

Hugh Laurie

It's a kind of spiritual snobbery that makes people think they can be happy without money.

Albert Camus

Happiness is the only good. The time to be happy is now. The place to be happy is here. The way to be happy is to make others so.

Robert Green Ingersoll

It's never too late - never too late to start over, never too late to be happy.

Jane Fonda

If only we'd stop trying to be happy we'd have a pretty good time.

Edith Wharton

People are basically the same the world over. Everybody wants the same things - to be happy, to be healthy, to be at least reasonably prosperous, and to be secure. They want friends, peace of mind, good family relationships, and hope that tomorrow is going to be even better than today.

Zig Ziglar

A table, a chair, a bowl of fruit and a violin; what else does a man need to be happy?

Albert Einstein

To be happy in this world, first you need a cell phone and then you need an airplane. Then you're truly wireless.

Ted Turner

I'm the type who'd be happy not going anywhere as long as I was sure I knew exactly what was happening at the places I wasn't going to. I'm the type who'd like to sit home and watch every party that I'm invited to on a monitor in my bedroom.

Andy Warhol

My personal goals are to be happy, healthy and to be surrounded by loved ones.

Kiana Tom

I've realized that being happy is a choice. You never want to rub anybody the wrong way or not be fun to be around, but you have to be happy. When I get logical and I don't trust my instincts - Thats when I get in trouble.

Angelina Jolie

I recognize that I have the ability to be selfish, but I also recognize that you can't be happy if you only care about yourself at the expense of other people.

Russell Brand

Often people ask how I manage to be happy despite having no arms and no legs. The quick answer is that I have a choice. I can be angry about not having limbs, or I can be thankful that I have a purpose. I chose gratitude.

Nick Vujicic

You know, God has a plan for me, and I'm going to follow in his footsteps and just rejoice and be happy.

Gabby Douglas

If you can do what you do best and be happy, you're further along in life than most people.

Leonardo DiCaprio

You can be happy where you are.

Joel Osteen

Research has shown that the best way to be happy is to make each day happy.

Deepak Chopra

As a teenager you are at the last stage in your life when you will be happy to hear that the phone is for you.

Fran Lebowitz

I never wanted to be rich or successful or famous. I just wanted to be happy and have fun.

Donna Leon

I'd rather be happy than right.

Marcus Brigstocke

It's like the old thing: The parents stay together for the kids, but the kids know that you don't want to be together. The kids would rather you be happy - and separate - than together and miserable. I don't want my kid to grow up around two parents who just don't work.

Jaime Pressly

If I had a place with a studio where I could paint I'd be happy.

Bruno Tonioli

I think people really want to be happy.

John Astin

People say: 'Oh, but would you be happy for your show to go on BBC3 if it was just online?' If I was sat here telling you I had just signed a huge deal with Netflix you'd be going: 'Wow, that's amazing.' You can't see it as 'Oh, it's no longer a channel because it's not on TV.'

James Corden

You see I found I didn't have to act to be happy.

Irene Dunne

I think people should be proud of the work they do, whatever it is. I have this other arty side that loves creating homes. I can be happy going to the hardware store.

Aida Turturro

More than 100 million women have worn my clothing and accessories,, and that's so fulfilling. My skincare line proves you don't have to spend a fortune to have beautiful skin. I've loved acting but if I never played another role and just focused on my business, I'd be happy.

Jaclyn Smith

I always would be happy to make a character even more unlikable, but you know, there's a limit and if you go there, you get into a very different kind of movie, man.

Paul Giamatti

I'm not sure the Russians would be happy that their iconic wooly mammoth has North American origins.

Hendrik Poinar

I don't pretend to be happy all the time. I think to be human is to be happy and unhappy by turns. But I have a great capacity to enjoy myself, and it seems to grow as I get older.

Diana Quick

Entrepreneurs cannot be happy people until they have seen their visions become the new reality across all of society.

Bill Drayton

Would I be happy just practicing law? No. Would I be happy just doing TV and speeches? No. I want to do all of these things and be as active as I can... but my main goal is to have some degree of influence on the public discussion.

Ed Rendell

As long as she is talented enough and passionate about doing it herself then I will be happy and support her. I think I will be sensible - my parents said I could only do it if I got my education and so I had something to fall back on.

Anna Friel

Some people can only be happy being a star. What happens if and when the work dries up?

Susan Hampshire

A hundred years ago, concerts were far more come-what-may - people played cards, drank beer and appreciated the music. If we go some way towards restoring that spirit, I'll be happy.

Charles Hazlewood

Through teaching myself how to be happy and get through things, I hope I can also do that for other people.

Taryn Manning

I've gotten e-mails asking, 'Are you taking students?' Well, come visit and I'll be happy to talk to you. But I'm not a degree-granting institution.

Antony Garrett Lisi

When I dropped out of high school at age 16, I didn't know I was going to become a writer - I just knew I'd never been happy in school, and I had this strong suspicion I'd be happy doing other things.

Philipp Meyer

What the purpose of my life is about is I want to become the kind of person that God wants me to become, and through my study of the scriptures I can articulate the kind of person that God would be happy if I become.

Clayton M. Christensen

I am not political. It is not my job. But I would be happy if politicians could read my work and draw some conclusions from it.

Thomas Piketty

I want to work and be happy.

Rickie Lee Jones

I would trade any writerly success if it would mean my children would be happy.

Mary Gordon

There are still civil rights issues. There are still people who can't be visited by their spouse in the hospital because they're gay. These are humanitarian issues. At the end of the day, all you want is for people to be happy in the pursuit of life, love and liberty.

Brandi Carlile

If I can't be happy, nobody can be happy.

Amanda Eliasch

I think when an actress marries she should leave the stage. She cannot be happy if she is married and remains on the stage. She must care more for her art or for her husband.

Billie Burke

I wasn't a great student. Just give me a school with no grades, and I'll be happy.

Alison Elliott

People who get to express their voice are paid by the people who make profit from it. So they're going to make you believe you have to spend your money buying these products otherwise you won't be happy. This is really wrong. Especially the implication it carries.

Michel Gondry

The best way to have your people be happy and satisfied is to earn the right to have them come back to work for you the next day, knowing that there are tons of other places.

Maynard Webb

I am a father, and I know the feel of being a father. Why wouldn't I want my gay friends to also be happy parents?

Juan Pablo Galavis

I respect every gay man and woman. They're that way, and they just want to be happy.

Juan Pablo Galavis

The art and culture that is New York, communications, finance, all these things help make up New York. The rest of the country should be happy that we are what we are.

David Dinkins

Yeah, I'd be happy to go back to Mexico or Japan to make another film.

Alex Cox

I love watching Hollywood movies - I just don't know if I'd be happy doing a 'Jurassic Park.'

Frances O'Connor

In general, you don't want to move your kids when they're teenagers. They're not going to be happy with you.

Jeremy Sisto

I'd be happy to do Star Trek again, if the writing was right.

Stephen Collins

I think and hope and believe that the Japanese government and the people of Japan will be happy and content with the progress of justice in this case and that it will not become a great issue in the future.

Howard Baker

I have dual citizenship; I would be happy to go to England. I would be very happy to go to America.

John McAfee

We, Britain and Germany, can neither of us be happy about our handling of the Iraq war.

Douglas Hurd

I've never done anything for money. My first love is things of limited commercial appeal. I could be happy doing Shakespeare for the rest of my life.

Karen Allen

If I am still doing what I'm doing and I still have respect in this town, haven't done anything completely and utterly stupid, then I'll be happy with myself.

Jeremy London

I would be happy at a piano bar, singing. I just want to home in on being the best singer I can be.

Debby Boone

I know that there's people that have expectations of me, and I'm a people pleaser, so I want them to be happy.

Yvette Nicole Brown

Ultimately, you choose to be happy or miserable. The reality is that although you are free to choose, you can't choose the consequences of your choices. They're preloaded. It's a package deal.

Sean Covey

Some younger drivers didn't grow up seeing racing as being dangerous. They break their little finger, and they are surprised. It's like, 'Be happy it's only that.'

Jacques Villeneuve

It's not right to believe that the only way you're gonna get a job and the only way you're gonna get a man or be happy is by being so skinny.

Maria Conchita Alonso

We should be happy. We should be enjoying that there is all this bounty. Somebody can take an iPod and have all the world's music at their beck and call in an instant. What an amazing thing!

Gregory Stock

The goal isn't to be successful; it's to be happy. And so it doesn't matter if I'm doing things in New York or teaching high school or I drop it altogether and sell coffee. The goal is to be happy, and people and relationships are what makes you happy.

Susan Egan

Well, here's what I'll say: The storytellers of 'Lost' have taken us on a pretty great journey, and there have been questions along the way, and criticisms along the way, but if you look at the totality of the show, or the experience of it as a whole, I think as long as you look at it from that perspective you'll be happy.

Daniel Dae Kim

There are times I wish I was more conventional. I would get a husband and a baby and a big SUV in the 'burbs and be happy. But forging my own way - my career, my relationships with wonderful but troubled people - that's who I am.

Lauren Oliver

I wanted to get out in the world, have a great job, make my mark, and see how far I could go. And I wanted to make good on the philosophy my mother drilled into us with all the subtlety of a Lady Gaga performance. I got it loud and clear. I would need to succeed, and then I could possibly be happy.

Karen Finerman

Until you can be happy, you can't facilitate happiness for anybody else.

Wendy Raquel Robinson

But, you know, I'd be happy just making music.

John Lurie

I'll be happy if I can gain even the smallest place inside the literary imagination of U.S. readers.

Elliot Perlman

We had our first meeting yesterday, and we just laughed all the way through, so if we can bottle that, then I'll be happy. We just get on, and that's half the battle.

Allan Carr

Being on 'Whitney' is a job, but stand-up is my life. I could never stop. There's an art to it. I love having strangers laugh with me, so as long as I can continue doing that, I'll be happy. Working on a show and collectively sharing ideas with a cast is great, but stand-up is my first love.

Chris D'Elia

I got into this business because I like acting and I want to make movies. I would be happy living the rest of my life never famous.

Scott Eastwood

You have to have a certain single-mindedness if you want to reach the top of the profession, and I'm not sure if I've got that cold-eyed egomania that perhaps is needed to get to the top. So as long as I can keep paying the mortgage and keep myself interested, I'll be happy.

David Harewood

I love music, and I love acting, so if I can just live and be able to do those two things, I can be happy, you know?

Craig Horner

Tell me who you want to see on the Left, and I'll hire them. If you give me a big name that's out there, that's floating around and wants work, I'd be happy to hire them.

Roger Ailes

A lot of actors think they can't be happy without the acting... But I think I couldn't be happy with it anymore.

Genie Francis

The Internet's a big enough place for everybody to be happy.

Ben Huh

If I'm home, I'll be happy. And if I'm around family, and if I'm working on projects with friends, I don't know what else I'd want to be doing.

Howard Warren Buffett

I don't think any child could really be happy between five and eight away from their parents.

Tina Louise

What I advise clients is, sell, pay the tax and be happy. Don't ask me to find a replacement unless it's land.

Mike Simpson

I don't look at things goin', 'Oh, is this gonna make me rich? Is this gonna make me a star? Am I gonna win awards?' If all that stuff happens, great. Who cares? I still have to wake up in the morning and go to work and be happy to do it.

Geoff Stults

I'm trying to do it my way. For me to be happy in the business means I have to do it myself.

Julian Cope

I think comfort, stability, and love are the things that really let me be happy. Deep down inside I'm a little boring, I guess.

Jeffrey Brown

Most of us are not real eager to grow, myself included. We try to be happy by staying in the status quo. But if we're not willing to be honest with ourselves about what we feel, we don't evolve.

Olympia Dukakis

You have to be a mindful eater. There has to be intention in what you do in your life if you're going to be happy and authentic. Food isn't supposed to be entertainment in the way that your kids, your work, and your relationship are.

Jorge Cruise

When you get the respect of the fans, it's very hard not to be happy.

Yaya Toure

Be happy with who you are, and know that being you is the best thing you can do for yourself.

Ellen Wong

I started to write as a child as soon as I could read, or even before, when my mother read me Beatrix Potter at bedtime. Writing seemed to me to be the only sensible way to live and be happy.

Jane Gardam

Psychologists say don't expect your life to be happy all the time. I go with the philosophy that every day can't be tops. Life is not like that - it's up and down.

Shirley Eaton

You don't have to have an eating disorder to be happy or successful.

Scarlett Pomers

So it doesn't have to be happy music to be inspiring.

Bela Fleck

They think the banjo can only be happy, but that's not true.

Bela Fleck

Only be an actor if you can't be happy doing anything else. I don't think you should be an actor if you want to be actor. I think you should be an actor if you have to be an actor.

Linden Ashby

I love working! I'm a huge fan of TV and will be happy as long as I'm getting to be creative.

Patrick Labyorteaux

My dad came over from Ireland when he was 13 and lived on the streets, working on building sites, and has just retired from his job delivering furniture for John Lewis. My mum has had the same job for 30 years as a sales assistant at Marks and Spencer. They've always been really great; they just want me to be happy.

Amanda Hale

Sometimes, it is precisely when you discover that you are living very happily that you suddenly find yourself in danger. To be happy means to discover that you are exposed to being hurt.

Siegfried Lenz

If someone has children, the first thing they want is for them to be happy, and then become someone in life and all that. But the educational system, I mean always, not just now, creates competitive, successful people, and does not educate them to be happy. The problem is that success gives money, not happiness. The eternal problem.

Jorge Bucay

All of us, who are members of the Germanic peoples, can be happy and thankful that once in thousands of years fate has given us, from among the Germanic peoples, such a genius, a leader, our Fuehrer Adolf Hitler, and you should be happy to be allowed to work with us.

Heinrich Himmler

Learn to enjoy every minute of your life. Be happy now. Don't wait for something outside of yourself to make you happy in the future. Think how really precious is the time you have to spend, whether it's at work or with your family. Every minute should be enjoyed and savored.

Earl Nightingale

It is not God's will merely that we should be happy, but that we should make ourselves happy.

Immanuel Kant

Most women would not be happy being me. People say, 'But you're alone.' But I don't feel alone. I feel very un-alone.

Stevie Nicks

I don't see how people are comfortable with seeing other people be great. You can be happy for anybody, but what is your excuse to not want to be great? These people are great because they just say, 'I'ma do that,' and they do it. That's it. There's no scientific process.

Kevin Hart

Desire nothing, give up all desires and be happy.

Swami Sivananda

To be happy at home is the ultimate result of all ambition, the end to which every enterprise and labor tends, and of which every desire prompts the prosecution.

Samuel Johnson

A productive employee who is kept busy working at his or her job is far more likely to be happy at that job and less likely to look for employment elsewhere.

Zig Ziglar

I have this really high priority on happiness and finding something to be happy about.

Taylor Swift

Happiness is an attitude of mind, born of the simple determination to be happy under all outward circumstances.

J. Donald Walters

I don't trip on that much. I just like to enjoy life and be happy.

Roy Ayers

Musical compositions can be very sad - Chopin - but you have the pleasure of this sadness. The cheap consolation is: you will be happy. The higher consolation is the pleasure and recognition of your unhappiness, the pleasure of having recognised that fate, destiny and life are such as they are and so you reach a higher form of consciousness.

Umberto Eco

Men can only be happy when they do not assume that the object of life is happiness.

George Orwell

It takes great wit and interest and energy to be happy. The pursuit of happiness is a great activity. One must be open and alive. It is the greatest feat man has to accomplish.

Robert Herrick

I have an odd theory on happiness, and it bothers people. My general theory is that happiness is a reward for an animal doing what it should be doing. So if a horse runs, it feels happy. Or if you are too thin, you can't be happy, because evolution wants you to be tense and anxious, trying to wake up in the morning looking for food.

James D. Watson

It is a kind of spiritual snobbery that makes people think they can be happy without money.

Albert Camus

I think women should start to embrace their age. What's the alternative to getting older? You die. I can't change the day I was born. But I can take care of my skin, my body, my mind, and try to live my life and be happy.

Olivia Munn

Happiness is not a brilliant climax to years of grim struggle and anxiety. It is a long succession of little decisions simply to be happy in the moment.

J. Donald Walters

It feels so good to be happy.

Etta James

My mother was suffering every day of her life, and what right did I have to be happy if she was suffering? So whenever I got happy about something, I felt the need to cut it off, and the only way to cut it off was to pray. 'Forgive me Lord.' For what, I didn't know.

Gene Wilder

Through our willingness to help others we can learn to be happy rather than depressed.

Gerald Jampolsky

To be happy, it first takes being comfortable being in your own shoes. The rest can work up from there.

Sophia Bush

No mother wants to hear her son say he's gay. Those two words rip the picture of a daughter-in-law and grandchildren into pieces. I felt sorry for my mom and wanted her to know everything was going to be all right. But then she said, 'I don't really care, Johnny, as long as I know that you are going to be happy.'

Johnny Weir

I am much obliged by the favourable sentiments you express towards me, and shall be happy if I can be of service in carrying into execution your plans.

George Stephenson

And when I look at my mother, I reflect on her strength and endurance. She's cranky sometimes, but she is lovable and loving. I'd be happy to be there at 86.

Lisa Scottoline

The sad thing is most people have to check with someone before they do the things that make them happy. We're all passing through; the least we can do is be happy, and the only way to do that is by being selfish.

Gene Simmons

We're constantly striving for success, fame and comfort when all we really need to be happy is someone or some thing to be enthusiastic about.

H. Jackson Brown, Jr.

It is possible to live happily in the here and the now. So many conditions of happiness are available - more than enough for you to be happy right now. You don't have to run into the future in order to get more.

Thich Nhat Hanh

I do not think I am successful just because I have money. I'm successful because I love who I am and I have no regrets, and I'm successful because I have a great heart and I have compassion and I care and I would be happy with or without money.

Suze Orman

The reason people find it so hard to be happy is that they always see the past better than it was, the present worse than it is, and the future less resolved than it will be.

Marcel Pagnol

Change is certain. Peace is followed by disturbances; departure of evil men by their return. Such recurrences should not constitute occasions for sadness but realities for awareness, so that one may be happy in the interim.

Percy Bysshe Shelley

When you wake up each morning, you can choose to be happy or choose to be sad. Unless some terrible catastrophe has occurred the night before, it is pretty much up to you. Tomorrow morning, when the sun shines through your window, choose to make it a happy day.

Lynda Resnick

Don't wish me happiness - I don't expect to be happy it's gotten beyond that, somehow. Wish me courage and strength and a sense of humor - I will need them all.

Anne Morrow Lindbergh

If we only wanted to be happy, it would be easy; but we want to be happier than other people, and that is almost always difficult, since we think them happier than they are.

Charles de Montesquieu

To be happy we must not be too concerned with others.

Albert Camus

We cannot be contented because we are happy, and we cannot be happy because we are contented.

Walter Savage Landor

Having good health, being able to breathe and be happy, that's one of the most beautiful gifts. On top of that, I have the gift to play music and make people happy through that. I'm just telling you from my heart, I'm so in love with life.

Roy Ayers

I won't be happy until we have every boy in America between the ages of six and sixteen wearing a glove and swinging a bat.

Babe Ruth

It isn't necessary to be rich and famous to be happy. It's only necessary to be rich.

Alan Alda

You do the right thing even if it makes you feel bad. The purpose of life is not to be happy but to be worthy of happiness.

Tracy Kidder

I can't hurt any more than I've been hurt, I can't cry any more than I've cried. I've been to the highest of highs and lowest of lows, so one day I'm going to find my middle ground and be happy.

Cheryl Cole

A man can be happy with any woman, as long as he does not love her.

Oscar Wilde

I can see, and that is why I can be happy, in what you call the dark, but which to me is golden. I can see a God-made world, not a manmade world.

Helen Keller

No one can be happy who has been thrust outside the pale of truth. And there are two ways that one can be removed from this realm: by lying, or by being lied to.

Lucius Annaeus Seneca

My decision to end my marriage was such a risk to lose ratings and lose my fan base. I had to take that risk for my inner peace and to be happy with myself.

Kim Kardashian

I just want to say to women, 'Be yourself - it's the inner beauty that counts. You are your own best friend, the key to your own happiness, and as soon as you understand that - and it takes a few heartbreaks - you can be happy.'

Cherie Lunghi

I am a positive person. I am not cynical. If you are born in this world, no matter who you are, negative things will happen. If you aren't positive as a person, you'll be very unhappy. It's extremely important to be positive, to laugh, to be happy, to accept life as it comes.

Bipasha Basu

I don't think there's anybody in this world who should be required to make you feel good about yourself. Be happy on your own.

Shahid Kapoor

It's time for me to do things I like so I will be happy, my wife will be happy, my friends will be happy. I just want to do something I'm proud of. It's time for me to change. I could sign with a company for 10 movies and I'm the king of video and so what?

Jean-Claude Van Damme

Until you are happy with who you are, you will never be happy because of what you have.

Zig Ziglar

Feeling sorry for ourselves is the most useless waste of energy on the planet. It does absolutely no good. We can't let our circumstances or what others do or don't do control us. We can decide to be happy regardless.

Joyce Meyer

I try to be a good daughter, as I believe in karma and feel that how you are with your parents is directly proportionate to what you receive in your life. I am a big oneness follower, and our gurus have told us that if you want to achieve external happiness, you need to be happy internally. And your inner circle is your family.

Shilpa Shetty

If there's one thing that makes me cynical, it's optimists. They are just far too cynical about cynicism. If only they could see that cynics can be happy, constructive, even fun to hang out with, they might learn a thing or two.

Julian Baggini

The problem is, I don't think I've got too much to offer at the minute. I'm busy working on myself. This sounds like real therapy talk, but it's like, you've got to be happy with yourself before you can go out and get yourself a girl.

Robbie Williams

We see the tendency in the world to criticise democracy and sometimes even to say that authoritarian countries like China are more efficient. That is very short-sighted. China looks efficient only because it can sacrifice most people's rights. This is not something the west should be happy about.

Ai Weiwei

To forget oneself is to be happy.

Robert Louis Stevenson

Puritanism. The haunting fear that someone, somewhere, may be happy.

H. L. Mencken

Wisdom allows nothing to be good that will not be so forever; no man to be happy but he that needs no other happiness than what he has within himself; no man to be great or powerful that is not master of himself.

Lucius Annaeus Seneca

Find me a man who's interesting enough to have dinner with and I'll be happy.

Lauren Bacall

You can't be happy by doing something groovy.

Bob Dylan

To be happy, make other people happy.

W. Clement Stone

I don't want to be stinky poo poo girl, I want to be happy flower child.

Drew Barrymore

Happiness includes chiefly the idea of satisfaction after full honest effort. No one can possibly be satisfied and no one can be happy who feels that in some paramount affairs he failed to take up the challenge of life.

Arnold Bennett

Sorrow happens, hardship happens, the hell with it, who never knew the price of happiness, will not be happy.

Yevgeny Yevtushenko

If I bring back only one gold people are going to say it's a disappointment. But not too many of them own an Olympic gold medal so if I get one I'm going to be happy.

Michael Phelps

It may sound too good to be true, but once you've seen the happiest people in your life who have nothing, you really start rethinking what the world, and society, tells us that we need to be happy.

Blake Mycoskie

It's my firm intention to whop cancer into submission and I truly believe I've given myself the best start possible by radically overhauling my diet and by staying true to my motto, which is: Don't worry, be happy, feel good. The first thing I did when I was diagnosed was to turn vegan.

Larry Hagman

If I can put on my album in a car or on my headphones and listen to the whole thing and love it, that's what I'm going to be happy putting out there.

Ed Sheeran

I'm a happy person, and I want everybody else to be happy. Nothing wrong with that.

Kenan Thompson

I know I will never be happy, but I know I can be gay!

Marilyn Monroe

I was brought up differently than the average American child because the average child is brought up expecting to be happy.

Marilyn Monroe

Any of us can be happy and have a good attitude when everything is going our way. But I believe it's the real test of your character and of your faith to say, 'Things are not going our way, but I'm still being good to people; I'm still attending church; I still have a good attitude.'

Joel Osteen

No man can be happy without a friend, nor be sure of his friend till he is unhappy.

Thomas Fuller

It is better that some should be unhappy rather than that none should be happy, which would be the case in a general state of equality.

Samuel Johnson

You can be happy, or you can be right. If you want to be part of a couple and win every argument, you're in trouble.

Steve Harvey

The human spirit needs to accomplish, to achieve, to triumph to be happy.

Ben Stein

As a vulnerability researcher, the greatest barrier I see is our low tolerance for vulnerability. We're almost afraid to be happy. We feel like it's inviting disaster.

Brene Brown

I'm a wonderful disaster. So are you. We're all a mess. We're in this culture that says take this pill and you'll be happy, go on this diet and you'll be thinner, have your teeth whitened, people will love you more.

Emilio Estevez

Confidence, as a teenager? Because I knew what I loved. I loved to read; I loved to listen to music; and I loved cats. Those three things. So, even though I was an only kid, I could be happy because I knew what I loved.

Haruki Murakami

To be happy is to be able to become aware of oneself without fright.

Walter Benjamin

Most of us believe in trying to make other people happy only if they can be happy in ways which we approve.

Robert Staughton Lynd

My ambition is to be happy.

Penelope Cruz

I don't know, I just want to be happy. I could be in a hole somewhere. Or I could completely lose it and be some hippy living in the woods with my dad.

Shia LaBeouf

I see it every day: People trying to create a home that somebody else tells them they should have. I don't care if it's a magazine or a bossy friend - when somebody says, 'This is what's elegant, this is what's trendy,' if it doesn't represent you, you're not going to be happy.

Nate Berkus

I'd be happy to be taken as a woman - and that's what I was initially trying to do when I started throwing on dresses and stuff. But that wasn't going to happen because everyone kept calling me sir. So I thought I'd change the method and just start wearing what I wanted to wear.

Eddie Izzard

The book 'Do You!' is about your inner voice. And when you connect to that voice then you - then the freedom comes. And we're only here to be happy. So happy makes money. Money doesn't make happy.

Russell Simmons

I want the people of the Philippines to be happy, even if they have nothing.

Manny Pacquiao

The great European dream was to diminish militant nationalism. We would all be happy Europeans together. But we are going to see the old monster of militant nationalism being awoken when people realise how little control their politicians have.

Antony Beevor

If you want to be happy for life, love what you do.

Mary Higgins Clark

I just want to be happy. You know what I'm saying? I just want to be happy, and I want to be able to make somebody else happy.

Sean Combs

Some people are going to be happy with my decision, some people aren't... But I must live my life.

Thomas Hearns

It is by not always thinking of yourself, if you can manage it, that you might somehow be happy. Until you make room in your life for someone as important to you as yourself, you will always be searching and lost.

Richard Bach

Indeed, man wishes to be happy even when he so lives as to make happiness impossible.

Saint Augustine

To be happy with a man you must understand him a lot and love him a little. To be happy with a woman you must love her a lot and not try to understand her at all.

Helen Rowland

My creed is that: Happiness is the only good. The place to be happy is here. The time to be happy is now. The way to be happy is to make others so.

Robert Green Ingersoll

The poor wish to be rich, the rich wish to be happy, the single wish to be married, and the married wish to be dead.

Ann Landers

Our words will either bring life and victory or death and destruction. If we want to be happy, we have to be serious about speaking words of life that line up with God's Word.

Joyce Meyer

In order that people may be happy in their work, these three things are needed: They must be fit for it. They must not do too much of it. And they must have a sense of success in it.

John Ruskin

Just try to be happy. Unhappiness starts with wanting to be happier.

Sam Levenson

Act happy, feel happy, be happy, without a reason in the world. Then you can love, and do what you will.

Dan Millman

I can say I'd honestly rather be happy than have 30 to 40 songs that I've written about these thrilling, exciting, horrible, unhappy times.

Taylor Swift

It is possible for a woman to be a romantic, but also to be single and to be happy.

Taylor Swift

A man is happy so long as he chooses to be happy and nothing can stop him.

Aleksandr Solzhenitsyn

Love one another and you will be happy. It's as simple and as difficult as that.

Michael Leunig

To live a life that is wrong for you is a form of dying. There are people who have lives that look perfect. They try to be happy, they believe they should be happy, they are trying to like it, but if it's off course from their north star, they aren't satisfied.

Martha Beck

I am not sure that it is of the first importance that you should be happy. Many an unhappy man has been of deep service to himself and to the world.

Woodrow Wilson

I sometimes wish I weren't as logical as I am and I wish I weren't as smart as I am, because I'd be happy.

Rush Limbaugh

The British do not expect happiness. I had the impression, all the time that I lived there, that they do not want to be happy; they want to be right.

Quentin Crisp

When you were born, you cried and everybody else was happy. The only question that matters is this - when you die, will you be happy when everybody else is crying?

Tony Campolo

My mom, she wasn't like a baseball mother who knew everything about the game. She just wanted me to be happy with what I was doing.

David Ortiz

I also learned that I love making money. Anyone who is not afraid of work will be happy with the money they make.

Gene Simmons

One of the things psychologists used to say was that if you are depressed, anxious or angry, you couldn't be happy. Those were at opposite ends of a continuum. I believe that you can be suffering or have a mental illness and be happy - just not in the same moment that you're sad.

Martin Seligman

The secret of happiness is the determination to be happy always, rather than wait for outer circumstances to make one happy.

J. Donald Walters

I just want to be happy, have kids, enjoy my life, help others and create some good work.

David Walliams

I'm going to be a happy housewife. I'm going to be washing boxers and cooking and doing all those sorts of housewife duties. I just want to be happy and proud of every single day.

Johnny Weir

Pop music thrives on repetition. You know a song's a hit when you've heard it so often that you'll be happy never to hear it again.

James Surowiecki

If I was on a march at the moment I would be saying to everyone: 'Be honest with each other. Admit there are limitless possibilities in relationships, and love as many people as you can in whatever way you want, and get rid of your inhibitions, and we'll all be happy.

Ian Mckellen

People are chasing cash, not happiness. When you chase money, you're going to lose. You're just going to. Even if you get the money, you're not going to be happy.

Gary Vaynerchuk

Creating ways to be happy is your life's work, a challenge that won't end until you die.

Martha Beck

I like college football, but I'm a huge college basketball fan. I could sit and watch every game of March Madness and be happy. That could be a vacation.

Lewis Black

I married a woman who is much better than me, I'm very fortunate to be with her and I know I'll be happy with her the rest of my life.

Jim Caviezel

You must understand, I don't have to be happy to be happy.

Juliette Binoche

I would be happy not even being a supermodel. Being able to get a taste of everything that I want a taste of makes me happy.

Summer Altice

To complete your daily mental hygiene, observe any part of you that is upset or anxious, and offer that part of yourself the following simple wishes: 'May you be well. May you be happy. May you be free from suffering.' Repeat this until you actually mean it.

Martha Beck

I've found that when the market's going down and you buy funds wisely, at some point in the future you will be happy. You won't get there by reading 'Now is the time to buy.'

Peter Lynch

I just want the fans of the book to be happy. I don't necessarily care about anyone else.

Kristen Stewart

I often look at women who wear great jeans and high heels and nice little T-shirts wandering around the city ,and I think, 'I should make more of an effort. I should look like that.' But then I think, 'They can't be happy in those heels.'

Kate Winslet

I think it's important to be happy before you can make anybody else happy.

Julianne Hough

The truth is, I just don't have the drive to be the prettiest and the thinnest. I can be happy for other people for their beauty.

Salma Hayek

You have a choice whether you want to be happy or not. I choose to be happy.

Vanessa Hudgens

I always had the theory that the most important thing is be happy, enjoy what are you doing, and be fresh mentally.

Rafael Nadal

When I heard that there were artists, I wished I could some time be one. If I could only make a rose bloom on paper, I thought I should be happy! Or if I could at last succeed in drawing the outline of winter-stripped boughs as I saw them against the sky, it seemed to me that I should be willing to spend years in trying.

Lucy Larcom

Having been let out of the barn once, I know I wouldn't be happy if I were home all the time.

Meryl Streep

If the movie is good then great, but if it's not then God, I feel so bad for that person with their face fifty feet tall, all blown up. Some people would be happy with that, that as long as their face was out there they're stoked about it. I'm not like that.

Kristen Stewart

I see nothing wrong with the human trait to desire. In fact, I consider it integral to our success mechanism. Becoming attached to what we desire is what causes the trouble. If you must have it in order to be happy, then you are denying the happiness of the here and now.

Peter McWilliams

I'm not really the party person. I don't 'become myself' once I'm drunk. I don't use alcohol to be happy.

Jessie J

It's a form of bullying, in my opinion, to make sure that your kid gets the best grades, the best jobs and all that sort of stuff. I just want my child to be happy. I want him to do his best and trust God in the rest, but I'm not going to bully him.

Nick Vujicic

Well, I think the golden rule I can think of is the fact that you must follow your passion and do something that's close to your heart. And I think that that's very important, well, to be successful and to be happy.

Kumar Mangalam Birla

I feel sorry sometimes for these sportsmen and women who put in just as much effort as the footballers. For example, athletes train at least as hard as footballers but have to be happy if they can earn enough to finance a decent education.

Angela Merkel

The soul of a woman is so important to maintain given all that is on our plates. Figuring out how to do it can be a little tricky. My prayer was, 'Lord, please help me. How can I do it all and not be overwhelmed? How can I do it all and still be happy?' His answer: Find the stolen moments of joy in all you do.

Niecy Nash

Any fool can be happy. What I'm interested in is satisfaction. There's got to be more to life than just being happy. You've got to be fulfilled. You've got to be satisfied; philosophically satisfied is what I mean.

Charlie Trotter

I would urge all bands that say they only care about credibility and don't care about money to send Gene Simmons every dollar that they don't want. I'd be happy to take it off them.

Gene Simmons

I try not to get too ahead of myself. I try to be happy where I am.

Miranda Lambert

For the last few years, it's been so chic for everybody to be miserable. Like if you're in with the cool crowd, you can't be happy.

Lenny Kravitz

Let us all be happy, and live within our means, even if we have to borrow the money to do it with.

Charles Farrar Browne

The more I travel around the world, the more I see people want the same thing - to be happy. We wouldn't be in a monetary system if we didn't have to work, so if my music can contribute to happiness, then that's my main responsibility.

Jason Mraz

Only a fool expects to be happy all the time.

Robertson Davies

The more people have, the less content they seem to be. In America, the cultural expectation that we're to be happy all the time and our children are to be happy all the time is toxic, and I think that really gets in the way of emotional well-being.

Andrew Weil

If the individual is to be happy in the contemporary order, he must be open-minded with respect to new values and new arrangements.

Thomas Cochrane

You choose to be happy, and in life we have as many good days as bad days. I try to find and record those songs that pull you through the bad days, and keep you believing that the good days are just around the corner.

Rodney Atkins

This is true enough, but success is the next best thing to happiness, and if you can't be happy as a success, it's very unlikely that you would find a deeper, truer happiness in failure.

Michael Korda

If I would be happy, I would be a very bad ball player. With me, when I get mad, it puts energy in my body.

Roberto Clemente

I am very happy in second-hand bookshops; would a gardener not be happy in a garden?

Hilary Mantel

My motivation and aspiration is the same, being number one or being number five. So that's the truth. And my goal is the same - it's to always be happy playing, it's to enjoy the game and improve always.

Rafael Nadal

I have to be creative to be happy.

Gwen Stefani

I say to the young, be happy that you were born in Italy because of the beauty of the human capital, both masculine and feminine, of this country... No other country has such human capital.

Rita Levi-Montalcini

Mother Nature made me the way I am, and I should be happy.

Karolina Kurkova

I never see my bad guys as simply bad. They want pretty much the same thing that you and I want: they want to be happy.

Elmore Leonard

I knew that I did not have to buy into society's notion that I had to be handsome and healthy to be happy. I was in charge of my 'spaceship' and it was my up, my down. I could choose to see this situation as a setback or as a starting point. I chose to begin life again.

Warren Mitchell

Money is not necessarily, although it helps a lot for happiness, it's not necessarily the best way to be happy, to be rich, you know.

Eric Ripert

I don't think there's a problem with being a teen idol, if that happens to me, I'll be happy to deal with it.

Josh Hartnett

I would be happy living on a massive ranch in Montana and not seeing anyone except my friends and family.

Nick Frost

Family, work, familiarity. Listen, if I had a magic wand and I could make myself really be happy, I'd zap me onto a farm. And I know nothing about farming.

Scott Baio

It's just really important I think for fashion to be affordable, because everyone should have the opportunity to wear cute things and be happy and comfortable in what they are wearing. That's definitely how I like to shop and how I like to think about clothes and fashion.

Lea Michele

I'm happy with who I am inside. I'd hate to have accolades and all that and not really be happy with who I was. So I'm really thankful for my family and for the support system that I have for being the person that I am today. I'm proud of who I am.

Keke Palmer

The reality is, if you have a high-level-energy dog, it's not going to be happy with a one-hour walk. Those types of dogs are going to require more than one hour of physical challenge in the outside world.

Cesar Millan

As a culture, I think we need to redefine what it means to be happy.

Tom Shadyac